The Little Book

of TENDERNESS

Illustrated by Alain Cancilleri

ixia
PRESS

Garden City, New York

Illustrated by Alain Cancilleri

Introduction by Emma Altomare

Translated by Iceigeo, Milan

WHITE STAR PUBLISHERS

WS White Star Publishers® is a registered
trademark property of White Star s.r.l.

Copyright

Copyright © 2018 by White Star s.r.l.
Piazzale Luigi Cadorna, 6
20123 Milan, Italy
www.whitestar.it
All rights reserved.

Bibliographical Note

This Ixia Press edition, first published in 2021, is a modified English translation of
A Book Full of Tenderness, originally published in Italian by White Star Publishers, Milan, in 2018.

International Standard Book Number

ISBN-13: 978-0-486-84817-4
ISBN-10: 0-486-84817-5

IXIA PRESS
An imprint of Dover Publications, Inc.

Manufactured in China by Leo Paper Group
84817501
www.doverpublications.com/ixiapress

2 4 6 8 10 9 7 5 3 1

2021

Introduction

What do we mean when we talk about tenderness? We don't always know or we're not always able to explain it because the world we live in continually teaches us that there is a time to be tender, when we are children, and a time to be strong, when we grow up and become adults. As if strength and tenderness were two completely opposite feelings that exclude one another—either you are strong or you are tender. Yet, not only can strength and tenderness live together side by side, they can be mutually nurturing. In fact, you can only become strong if you have the freedom to experience every emotion that lives inside you, to put it on and show it to the rest of the world. So perhaps we simply need to learn to practice tenderness a bit more, because the Italian poet Alda Merini was right when she wrote: "We are hungry for tenderness . . . . We need these small gestures that make us feel good."

When I approach a child, he inspires in me two sentiments; tenderness for what he is, and respect for what he may become.

—Louis Pasteur

An infinite benevolence lay in that gaze:
tenderness, compassion, the empty,
fatuous profundity of a lover.

—Patrick Süskind

Friendship is a word, the very sight of which in print makes the heart warm.

—Augustine Birrell

Tenderness is the repose of passion.

—Joseph Joubert

All real men are gentle; without
tenderness, a man is uninteresting.

—Marlene Dietrich

Sweetness gets more than violence.

—Jean de La Fontaine

What do we live for, if it is not to make life less difficult to each other?

—George Eliot

The hardness of these times must not make us lose the tenderness of our hearts.

—Che Guevara

Beauty, madam, pleases the eyes only;
sweetness of disposition charms the soul.

— Voltaire

We have a great deal more kindness than is ever spoken.

— Ralph Waldo Emerson

At the end of your life, you will never regret not having passed one more test, not winning one more verdict, or not closing one more deal. You will regret time not spent with a husband, a child, a friend, or a parent.

—Barbara Bush

Thank you for Tenderness. I find
it is the only food that the Will takes,
nor that from general fingers.

—Emily Dickinson

There is not only need for tenderness, there is also need to be tender for the other: we shut ourselves up in a mutual kindness, we mother each other reciprocally; we return to the root of all relations, where need and desire join.

—Roland Barthes

What I was trying to show was a world where I would feel good, where people would be kind, where I would find the tenderness I hoped to receive. My photos were like the proof that this world can exist.

—Robert Doisneau

We are hungry for tenderness . . . .
We need these small gestures
that make us feel good.

—Alda Merini

Nothing makes the earth seem so spacious
as to have friends at a distance; they make
the latitudes and longitudes.

—Henry David Thoreau

There is only one happiness in life,
to love and be loved.

—George Sand

The only beautiful eyes are those that look at you with tenderness.

—Coco Chanel

The rain has a vague secret of tenderness,
something resignedly and amiably somnolent.

—Federico García Lorca

Our greatest strength lies in the gentleness and tenderness of our heart.

— Rumi

There is no charm equal
to tenderness of heart.

—Jane Austen

There is nothing so strong as that real loving kindness, and nothing so tender as that genuine strength.

—St. Francis de Sales

Tenderness and kindness are not
signs of weakness and despair,
but manifestations
of strength and resolution.

—Khalil Gibran

Kindness is tenderness. Kindness is love,
but perhaps greater than love. . . .
Kindness is good will. Kindness says,
"I want you to be happy."

— Randolph Ray

To be soft is to be powerful.

— Rupi Kaur

How strange that each tenderness was
precisely the tenderness most craved.

—Emily Dickinson

We are afraid to care too much, for fear
that the other person does not care at all.

—Eleanor Roosevelt

What tigress is there that does not purr
over her young ones and fawn upon them
in tenderness?

—St. Augustine

How far you go in life depends upon your
being tender with the young, compassionate
with the aged, sympathetic with the striving,
and tolerant of the weak and strong.
Because someday in your life
you will have been all of these.

—George Washington Carver

The prudence of the best heads
is often defeated by the tenderness
of the best hearts.

—Henry Fielding

It's the great mystery of human life that old grief passes gradually into quiet tender joy.

— Fyodor Dostoyevsky

I have learned that to be with those I like
is enough.

—Walt Whitman

I've discovered if you treat people the way
you wish to be treated at all times, you will
get exactly what the universe has intended.

—Oprah Winfrey

You can't substitute material things for love or for gentleness or for tenderness or for a sense of comradeship.

—Mitch Albom

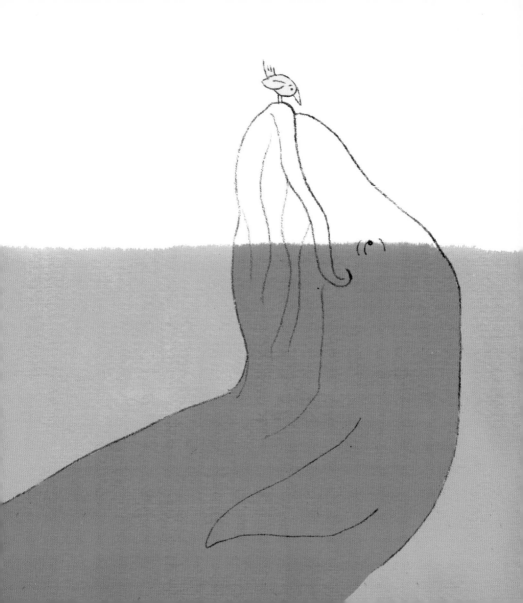

There never was any heart truly
great and generous, that was not
also tender and compassionate.

— Robert Frost

Let us care for one another and
let us be loving custodians of creation.

—Pope Francis

The people I find irresistible

are those in whom the child was not killed.

The qualities of openness,

trust, inquisitiveness, tenderness,

eagerness, enthusiasm,

others undefinable, come from the child

in us and are the source of charm.

—Anaïs Nin

Be a rainbow in someone else's cloud.

—Maya Angelou

There was nothing more complete than time-tested love, a couple journeying together and welcoming the gradual evolution of passion into tenderness.

—Marc Levy

Nobody has ever measured, not even poets, how much the heart can hold.

—Zelda Fitzgerald

But I've never heard words like this
in the night
(Where does such tenderness come from?)
with my head on your chest, rest.

—Marina Tsvetaeva

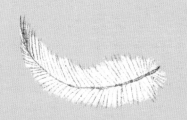

A mother's arms are made of tenderness and children sleep soundly in them.

—Victor Hugo

A simple smile, a tender touch,
speaks the true language of love.

—Dan Fogelberg

The most important medicine is tender love and care.

—Mother Teresa

Kindness in words creates confidence.

Kindness in thinking creates profoundness.

Kindness in giving celebrates love.

—Lao Tzu

Oh, that gentleness!

how far more potent is it than force!

—Charlotte Brontë